Tools

Search
Notes

Discuss

MyReportLinks.com Books
Go!

STATES

TENNESSEE

A MyReportLinks.com Book

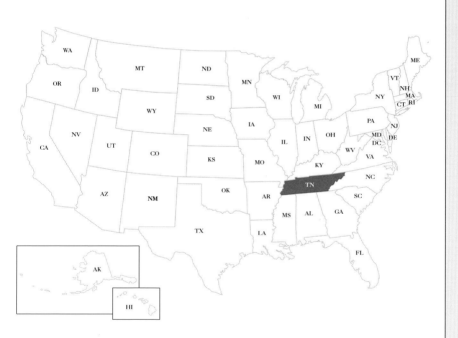

Ron Knapp

MyReportLinks.com Books

an imprint of

Enslow Publishers, Inc.

Box 398, 40 Industrial Road
Berkeley Heights, NJ 07922
USA

For Helen LaBar

MyReportLinks.com Books, an imprint of Enslow Publishers, Inc. MyReportLinks is a trademark of Enslow Publishers, Inc.

Library of Congress Cataloging-in-Publication Data

Knapp, Ron.
  Tennessee / Ron Knapp.
    p. cm. — (States)
Summary: Discusses the land and climate, economy, government, and history of the state of Tennessee. Includes Internet links to Web sites.
Includes bibliographical references (p.) and index.
  ISBN 0-7660-5120-X
  1. Tennessee—Juvenile literature. [1. Tennessee.] I. Title. II.
States (Series : Berkeley Heights, N.J.)
  F436.3 .K57 2003
  976.8—dc21
                    2002154289

Printed in the United States of America

10 9 8 7 6 5 4 3 2 1

To Our Readers:
Through the purchase of this book, you and your library gain access to the Report Links that specifically back up this book.
The Publisher will provide access to the Report Links that back up this book and will keep these Report Links up to date on **www.myreportlinks.com** for three years from the book's first publication date.
We have done our best to make sure all Internet addresses in this book were active and appropriate when we went to press. However, the author and the Publisher have no control over, and assume no liability for, the material available on those Internet sites or on other Web sites they may link to.
The usage of the MyReportLinks.com Books Web site is subject to the terms and conditions stated on the Usage Policy Statement on **www.myreportlinks.com**.
A password may be required to access the Report Links that back up this book. The password is found on the bottom of page 4 of this book.
Any comments or suggestions can be sent by e-mail to comments@myreportlinks.com or to the address on the back cover.

Photo Credits: © Corel Corporation, pp. 3, 10 (flag); © 1995 PhotoDisc, p. 41; © 2001 National Civil Rights Museum, p. 45; © 2002 The Nature Conservancy, p. 20; © 2003 Elvis Presley Enterprises, Inc., pp. 16, 25; Enslow Publishers, Inc., pp. 1, 22–23; James K. Polk Memorial Association, p. 34; Library of Congress, pp. 31, 32; Photo by Ira Lupkin, p. 17; State of Tennessee Photo Services, pp. 11, 14; Tennessee Tourist Development, pp. 13, 19, 27, 28, 37, 39; Tennessee Valley Authority, p. 43; The Hermitage: Home of President Andrew Jackson, pp. 24, 33; Women's Basketball Hall of Fame, p. 29.

Cover Photo: Corbis

Cover Description: Nashville

Contents

MyReportLinks.com Books
Great Books, Great Links, Great for Research!

MyReportLinks.com Books present the information you need to learn about your report subject. In addition, they show you where to go on the Internet for more information. The pre-evaluated Report Links that back up this book are kept up to date on **www.myreportlinks.com**. With the purchase of a MyReportLinks.com Books title, you and your library gain access to the Report Links that specifically back up that book. The Report Links save hours of research time and link to dozens—even hundreds—of Web sites, source documents, and photos related to your report topic.

Please see "To Our Readers" on the Copyright page for important information about this book, the MyReportLinks.com Books Web site, and the Report Links that back up this book.

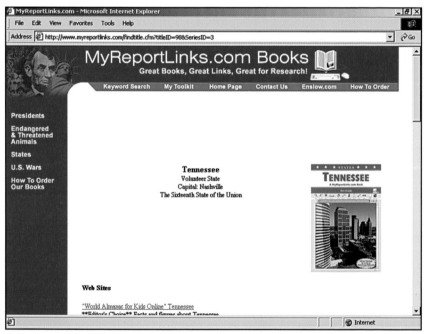

Access:

The Publisher will provide access to the Report Links that back up this book and will try to keep these Report Links up to date on our Web site for three years from the book's first publication date. Please enter **STN6836** if asked for a password.

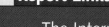
Report Links

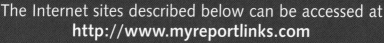

The Internet sites described below can be accessed at
http://www.myreportlinks.com

*EDITOR'S CHOICE

▶ *World Almanac for Kids Online:* **Tennessee**
The *World Almanac for Kids Online* provides essential information
about Tennessee. Here you will learn about land and resources,
population, education, government and politics, economy, history,
and much more.

Link to this Internet site from http://www.myreportlinks.com

*EDITOR'S CHOICE

▶ **Explore the States: Tennessee**
America's Story from America's Library, a Library of Congress Web site,
tells the story of Tennessee. Here you will learn interesting facts about
the Volunteer State and the real birthplace of country music.

Link to this Internet site from http://www.myreportlinks.com

*EDITOR'S CHOICE

▶ **US Census Bureau: Tennessee**
The U.S. Census Bureau Web site provides quick facts about
Tennessee. Included is information about overall population,
business-related statistics, and geography.

Link to this Internet site from http://www.myreportlinks.com

*EDITOR'S CHOICE

▶ **Country Music Hall of Fame**
Take a virtual tour of the Country Music Hall of Fame, located in
Tennessee. Read its history, see historic photos, and read the latest
news in country music. See a list of those inducted to the Hall.

Link to this Internet site from http://www.myreportlinks.com

*EDITOR'S CHOICE

▶ **The Tennessee State Museum**
Learn a bit of Tennessee history at this Web site. Here you can view the
permanent and temporary exhibits of this museum. You will also see
photos of actual artifacts and read some interesting facts.

Link to this Internet site from http://www.myreportlinks.com

*EDITOR'S CHOICE

▶ **TennesseeAnytime**
The official Web site of Tennessee provides information about
government, education, employment, facts and records, and much
more. A great place to begin your research.

Link to this Internet site from http://www.myreportlinks.com

Report Links

The Internet sites described below can be accessed at
http://www.myreportlinks.com

▶ **American Roots Music**

Learn the history of music in America. Included is a history of the
fiddle and other musical instruments that were brought by the earliest
settlers to Tennessee.

Link to this Internet site from http://www.myreportlinks.com

▶ **Blue Ridge Highlander**

Read about the natural beauty of the Blue Ridge Mountains, including the
history and culture of the mountain communities. You will also find photos
and stories.

Link to this Internet site from http://www.myreportlinks.com

▶ **Elvis: Official Site**

Elvis Presley is still known as "The King of Rock 'n' Roll." Read his
colorful biography that spans his life—from his humble beginnings—to
his rise to world fame. This site contains a full discography, filmography,
and a list of television appearances.

Link to this Internet site from http://www.myreportlinks.com

▶ **Great Smoky Mountains National Park**

Read the history of the Great Smoky Mountains National Park in Tennessee
and North Carolina. Learn about Cade's Cove, once known as "place of the
river otter" to the Cherokee. Click on "InDepth" to learn more.

Link to this Internet site from http://www.myreportlinks.com

▶ **The History of Rock 'N' Roll: Rockabilly**

Ever wonder where "rockabilly" came from? Read the history of this blend of
hillbilly and rock music that was born in Tennessee. See how Elvis, Scotty
Moore, and Bill Black had a hand in its beginnings.

Link to this Internet site from http://www.myreportlinks.com

▶ **International Bluegrass Music Association**

This site reveals the many different musical influences that went into creating
bluegrass, including gospel music.

Link to this Internet site from http://www.myreportlinks.com

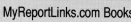
Report Links

 The Internet sites described below can be accessed at
http://www.myreportlinks.com

▶**Live from Austin: The Story of Davy Crockett**
View this time line of the life of legendary frontiersman Davy
Crockett. This biography takes readers through his childhood,
the Creek Indian War, and the Alamo.

Link to this Internet site from http://www.myreportlinks.com

▶**Memphis Guide**
Learn about the city of Memphis at this site, including the significance
of Beale Street, which many consider the birthplace of blues music.

Link to this Internet site from http://www.myreportlinks.com

▶**Nashville Public Library: Who's Who in Nashville History**
View this listing of short biographies of notable people in Nashville
history. Learn about the "Boy Hero of the Confederacy" as well as
the inventor of Maxwell House Coffee. Do you know who gave the
American flag the nickname "Old Glory?" You will after you read this!

Link to this Internet site from http://www.myreportlinks.com

▶**National Civil Rights Museum**
The National Civil Rights Museum is located in Memphis, Tennessee.
Read the history of the civil rights movement, including speeches and
news. See a list of Freedom Award winners, including Nelson Mandela.

Link to this Internet site from http://www.myreportlinks.com

▶**The Nature Conservancy: Tennessee**
View photos of the Hatchie River, Shady Valley Bog, and the
Cumberland Plateau as you learn how this organization works to
conserve "the Last Great Places" in Tennessee. Take a virtual nature
hike, too!

Link to this Internet site from http://www.myreportlinks.com

▶**Opry.com**
At this site you can read the interesting history of the Grand Ole Opry;
just click on "history." You can also view images and watch video clips
of today's Opry performers.

Link to this Internet site from http://www.myreportlinks.com

Report Links

 The Internet sites described below can be accessed at
http://www.myreportlinks.com

▶ River of Song

At the River of Song Web site you will find a time line of Tennessee's musical history. You will also learn about the similarities and differences between blues and gospel music.

Link to this Internet site from http://www.myreportlinks.com

▶ Rock City

Take a virtual tour of this famous Tennessee landmark. See photos of Rock City and view a gallery of barns that people have used over the years to encourage others to see this wonder.

Link to this Internet site from http://www.myreportlinks.com

▶ Sequoyah

At this site you will learn all about Sequoyah and how he developed an alphabet for his people. There is even a picture of the alphabet.

Link to this Internet site from http://www.myreportlinks.com

▶ Stately Knowledge: Tennessee

Find facts about Tennessee, including information about the capital, current governor, motto, and state symbols. Includes a map of the United States with the state of Tennessee highlighted.

Link to this Internet site from http://www.myreportlinks.com

▶ Tennessee

The Netstate Web site offers information about Tennessee symbols, people, history, geographical statistics, climate information, and definitions of geographical terms. You will learn that the highest point in Tennessee is "Clingman's Dome."

Link to this Internet site from http://www.myreportlinks.com

▶ Tennessee Aquarium

Tennessee Aquarium is the world's largest. See a photo of this massive building and learn interesting facts of what the aquarium has to offer. Read about their efforts to save the seahorse.

Link to this Internet site from http://www.myreportlinks.com

Report Links

 The Internet sites described below can be accessed at
http://www.myreportlinks.com

▶**The Tennessee Presidents Trust**
The Tennessee Presidents Trust Web site provides brief biographies of
Andrew Jackson, James K. Polk, and Andrew Johnson.

Link to this Internet site from http://www.myreportlinks.com

▶**Tennessee State Library**
Check out this site to learn about Tennessee genealogy and history,
including census and vital records. Under "archives" there is a link to
"images from the past" that contains digitized historical photos.

Link to this Internet site from http://www.myreportlinks.com

▶**Tennessee Valley Authority**
Check out the link to "TVA Kids" where you can learn about solar
power, wildlife, environmental conservation, electricity, and the
waterways of the Tennessee Valley.

Link to this Internet site from http://www.myreportlinks.com

▶**USDA Forest Service Southern Region:**
Cherokee National Forest
Learn about Tennessee's only national forest. Read of its natural
recourses, forest planning, and forest history. Photos of the forest
and wildlife are included.

Link to this Internet site from http://www.myreportlinks.com

▶**Women's Basketball Hall of Fame**
The Women's Basketball Hall of Fame is located in Knoxville,
Tennessee. See a list of inductees, and read a history of the Hall.
View a time line of the history of basketball. Photos are included.

Link to this Internet site from http://www.myreportlinks.com

▶**Women in History: Wilma Rudolph Biography**
Read this biography of a woman from Tennessee who overcame illness
and racial and gender barriers to become an Olympic gold medallist
and one of the most-celebrated female athletes of all time.

Link to this Internet site from http://www.myreportlinks.com

Tennessee Facts

Capital
Nashville

Gained Statehood
June 1, 1796, the
sixteenth state

Population
5,689,283*

Counties
95

Bird
Mockingbird

Tree
Tulip poplar

Flower
Iris

Animal
Raccoon

Amphibian
Tennessee cave salamander

Reptile
Box turtle

Butterfly
Zebra swallowtail

Gem
Tennessee river pearl

Songs
Tennessee has six state songs[1]

Motto
Agriculture and Commerce

Nickname
Volunteer State

Flag
In the center of a red field is
a blue circle containing three
white stars. The three stars
represent the unity of the
East, Middle, and West divi-
sions of the state. The outer
edge of the blue circle is
white. Trimming the right
edge of the flag is a thin
white stripe followed by a
thicker blue stripe.

*Population reflects the 2000 census.

The Music of Tennessee

For more than two centuries, people around the world have been tapping their toes, dancing, and singing to the music of Tennessee. The earliest settlers from Great Britain found American Indians living in Tennessee playing ancient songs on drums and rattles. The settlers brought fiddles to play and ballads to sing. Whenever people got together for weddings, parties, or even funerals, they wound up listening and dancing to fiddle music.

Slaves from Africa brought their own music to Tennessee. Emotional, sometimes even mournful singing, combined with strong rhythm and steady, heavy beats. Singing was something African Americans could do to pass the time as they worked long hours in the fields.

Religious, or gospel, music was popular among both blacks and whites. In Tennessee, religious music was never quiet or boring. The congregations always sang loudly and with great spirit.

Then, early in the 1900s, other instruments joined the fiddle. Inexpensive guitars,

A three-man band plays at ▶ the Museum of Appalachia in Knoxville, Tennessee. They are using instruments commonly heard in the music of the region.

banjos, and mandolins could be purchased from salesmen or catalogs.

Bluegrass Music

With the new instruments almost anybody could become a musician. Groups of friends formed string bands. Fiddles, guitars, banjos, and sometimes mandolins combined to form a unique sound. Sometimes one of the instruments was a steel guitar, with its distinctive, tinny sound.

The bands' singers joined their voices in elaborate harmonies. Usually they sang in high-pitched nasal voices.

Such bands produced a new type of sound, called "bluegrass," which was named after the plant that covered the hills in neighboring Kentucky where the music was given its name.

Recording the Music

Ralph Peer brought early mobile sound-recording music to Bristol, Tennessee, in 1927. In just ten days, he recorded seventy-six songs performed by nineteen groups. Soon Tennessee's music was not just being enjoyed by the musicians, their families, and friends. It was being purchased and played by people all across the country.

Peer discovered two of the most important acts in country music. Jimmie Rodgers was a Mississippi railroad worker who blended the hard sound of African-American blues music with country yodeling. Two of his biggest hits were "Mule Skinner Blues" and "T. for Texas."

A. P. Carter decided that making music was more fun than selling fruit trees so he picked up a fiddle and put a band together. A woman had never before been the lead singer in a country band, but Carter chose his wife, Sara, to handle vocals and play the auto harp. Sara's cousin,

Maybelle, completed the band with her steady, punchy guitar playing. They called themselves the Carter Family. The Carter's blew out eight tires during the long drive from their home in Virginia to Peer's recording session in Bristol. As soon as they arrived, they recorded music that is still enjoyed today. "The Storms Are on the Ocean" was one of their most popular recordings.

On the Radio—And Beyond

In the 1920s, Americans began buying millions of radios. For the first time they could hear news, music, comedy, and drama broadcast from cities far away.

One of the earliest programs, the *WSM Barn Dance* on Nashville station WSM, began in 1925. The first performer was eighty-year-old Uncle Jimmy Thompson. He bragged that he could "fiddle the bugs off a 'tater vine."[1] The show featured such colorful acts as Dr. Humphrey Bate

The Grand Ole Opry continues to be the world's longest-running, live radio show. Shortly after its inception, people came from all over to see the live performance.

and the Possum Hunters, the Fruit Jar Drinkers, Uncle Dave Macon, and the Gully Jumpers.

Southern comedians told jokes and stories between musical sets. *Barn Dance* became a popular program. It grew from one hour to three hours, and WSM increased its broadcasting power so it could be heard all over the Midwest.

In 1928, the show changed its name—by accident. The program before *Barn Dance* was an hour of classical and opera music. George D. Hay, the WSM announcer, opened his show by announcing, "We have been listening to music taken largely from Grand Opera. From now on we will present the Grand Ole Opry."[2]

One of the show's most popular performers over the years was Roy Acuff, who sang with the Smoky Mountain Boys. "The Wabash Cannonball" was his biggest record. The show's most enduring comedy act was Minnie Pearl, who always appeared wearing a big hat with the price tag still attached.

The Grand Ole Opry was one of the most popular radio programs in the country, and it was still successful at the start of the twenty-first century. It has helped launch the careers of many successful country artists.

Beale Street, located in Memphis, Tennessee, is famous for bringing together all the different kinds of music originating in the region—delta blues, rock 'n' roll, jazz, gospel, and R&B.

In 1972, the owners of the Grand Ole Opry opened a huge amusement park in Nashville, called Opryland. Country music has now spread from the hills of Tennessee all over the world. Acts such as Johnny Cash, Dolly Parton, Garth Brooks, and the Dixie Chicks have sold millions of recordings. In 2002, *O, Brother, Where Art Thou?*, a collection of bluegrass and "old time" music, won the Grammy award for Album of the Year.

Not Just Country

If Nashville is Music City, USA, for country music fans, Memphis is the home of the blues. The blues rely on sad, brassy sounds to set the mood. The lyrics almost always tell hard luck stories.

W. C. Handy moved to Memphis when he was a young man in 1908. He was a teacher and a factory worker who loved to play the cornet. He and his band played on Beale Street. Soon he was composing his own tunes, songs such as "Memphis Blues," "Beale Street Blues," and "St. Louis Blues."

Handy's work brought blues music to the attention of millions of listeners. Some of the world's best blues music is still played in the clubs along Beale Street. The annual Beale Street Music Festival draws thousands of fans.

The King of Rock 'n' Roll

Early in the 1950s, Elvis Presley was a quiet teenager in Memphis who loved music. He listened to blues and country and visited African-American churches to witness the excitement of gospel.

Presley combined those types of music into his own style. Elvis's style was unique. He dyed his hair black and slicked it down. He grew his sideburns to the bottom of his

ears. When he sang, he danced and wiggled. Not everyone knew what to make of him or his music at first. Many radio stations would not play his early records because he sounded like an African American. They wanted to make sure they played only "white music." The Grand Ole Opry hired Presley, but he only lasted a day. Whatever his music was, the owners decided, it was not country. Some called it "rockabilly." A little bit hillbilly, or country, with some rock 'n' roll thrown in.

When the world finally got a chance to hear Presley's records, popular music changed forever. His wild, exciting style with its driving beat pushed his records to the top of

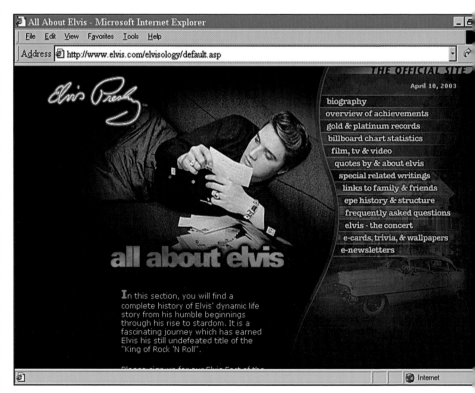

▲ *Elvis Presley has sold over one billion records worldwide. That is more than anyone in record industry history. In America alone, he has had 140 albums and singles certified as either gold, platinum, or multi-platinum.*

Music fans can tour Sun Studios in Memphis, where Elvis first recorded with other rock pioneers such as Scotty Moore. Shown here is one of Scotty Moore's guitars.

the charts everywhere. After Elvis came along, rock music dominated the charts.

For years, Elvis was one of the most successful and popular singers in the world. Most experts consider Presley's earliest hits such as "Hound Dog," "Jailhouse Rock," and "Heartbreak Hotel" classics of rock 'n' roll music. More than a quarter century since his death in 1977, when someone mentions "The King of Rock and Roll," everybody knows that is Presley. His albums still can sell millions of copies. His home, Graceland, is one of the nation's top tourist attractions. In March 2002, a collection of thirty of Presley's hits reached No. 1 on the album charts thirty-five years after his death.[3]

People and the Land

According to the 2000 United States census, 80.2 percent of Tennessee's 5,689,283 people are white. African Americans, with 16.4 percent, are the largest minority group. Hispanic Americans make up only 2.2 percent of the total.

Tennessee is growing. From 1990 to 2000, its population increased by 16.7 percent. The national population increased by just 13.1 percent.

Based on 1997 census estimates, the state's median household income is $32,047, just about $5,000 less than the national median total of $37,005.

▶ Government

Tennessee's state government is centered in the capital city of Nashville. The structure of the state government is not unique. Like all the other states, as well as the United States federal government, it has three branches.

The governor heads the executive branch. He or she appoints most of state government's department heads.

The legislative branch includes the General Assembly, which is compromised of the ninety-nine-member house of representatives and the thirty-three-member senate. The Assembly meets every year and is responsible for making laws.

At the top of the judicial branch is the state supreme court. There is also a court of appeals and many chancery, criminal, juvenile, and municipal courts.

△ Fort Nashborough was built by James Robertson and John Donelson in the winter of 1779–80. In 1784, its name was changed to Nashville. Although Tennessee entered the Union on June 1, 1796, it was not until 1843 that the city became the state capital.

▶ Geography

Tennessee has an interesting variety of geographical regions. In the east is the Blue Ridge region. This is a thin strip of mountains located along the border with North Carolina. It is the highest area in the state, with an average elevation of about five thousand feet.

Located farther west is the Appalachian Ridge and Valley region. The land gradually slopes down from the mountains. The valleys have good soil for farming.

Most of Tennessee's coal is found in the Cumberland Plateau, a relatively high, flat area that lies next to the valleys.

△ Much of the Cumberland Plateau's biodiversity is preserved by four Tennessee state parks—Fall Creek Falls, Cumberland Mountain, Cumberland Trail, and South Cumberland state parks—as well as national reserves, such as Big South Fork National River and Recreation Area.

The Highland Rim is a hilly area with steep slopes. It surrounds the Nashville (or Central) Basin, the state's best area for farming. Wheat, tobacco, potatoes, and tomatoes grow well there.

The Gulf Coastal Plain is a flat region stretching between the Mississippi and Tennessee Rivers. The lowest part of the state is the strip along the Mississippi River bordering Missouri and Arkansas.

Climate

In the summer, Tennessee is a warm, humid place. The average high temperature in July is around 90°F. The low temperature in January averages around 30°F. No matter the season, the eastern Blue Ridge and Appalachian regions usually are cooler than the rest of the state.

The Cumberland Plateau gets slightly more rain than the rest of the state. Most areas average about fifty-two inches of precipitation a year.

Economy

More people in Tennessee are employed in service jobs than in anything else. About 70 percent of the state's gross product comes from the service industry. Service jobs include work for governments, hospitals, banks, stores, and delivery services.

Manufacturing accounts for about 24 percent of Tennessee's gross state product. Many factories make heating, refrigeration, and transportation equipment. No state produces more chemicals than Tennessee.

Most of the state's agricultural income comes from beef and milk. The most important crops are soybeans, cotton, corn, and tobacco.

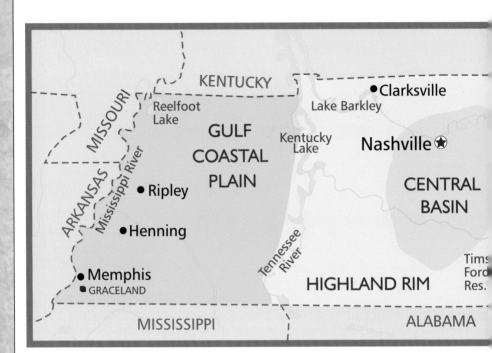

▲ A map of Tennessee.

There is some mining, mostly of coal, and the timber industry is still important.

▶ The Cities

Memphis, Tennessee's largest city, is located on the banks of the Mississippi River in the southwest corner of the state. Memphis was founded in 1819. The Mississippi River reminded the settlers of the Nile River, so they named the new city after Memphis, an ancient city on the Nile in Egypt. It had a population of 650,100 in the year 2000.

The capital and second largest city is Nashville, with 569,891 people. Nashville is located in the center of the state. Nashville was founded in 1780 by settlers from

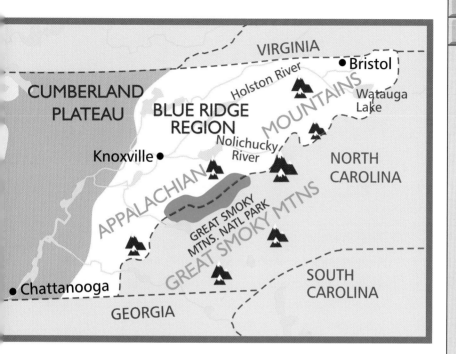

Virginia. The residents named it after Francis Nash, a Revolutionary War hero.

Knoxville, with 173,890 people, was established in 1786. Its name honors Henry Knox, the first United States secretary of war. Knoxville was built along the Tennessee River in the eastern part of the state. The city is the home of the University of Tennessee–Knoxville, the largest university in the state with about twenty-five thousand students. Known as the Volunteers, the Tennessee sports teams are known for winning national championships in football and women's basketball.

Chattanooga is a Cherokee Indian word meaning "rock coming to a point." It was called Ross's Landing when it was settled in 1815, and renamed Chattanooga in 1838. With a population of 155,554, it is located in southeastern Tennessee.

Chapter 3

Attractions

People who like music, history, the land's natural beauty, sports, or even amusement parks, are drawn to Tennessee. Two of its most popular attractions are the homes of two of its most famous citizens.

▷ The Hermitage

Andrew Jackson was an orphan who grew up to be president of the United States. Along the way, he became a wealthy man. His mansion, the Hermitage, located near Nashville, was one of Tennessee's most beautiful homes.

The paintings, tools, furniture, and cooking utensils are almost all original items used by the Jackson family. Scattered around the grounds are hickory trees—very appropriate for the home of the man known as Old Hickory. Also on the grounds is a formal garden set up very much as it was when Jackson's wife, Rachel, lived there. In the corner of

◁ Andrew Jackson retired to his home, the Hermitage, after his presidency. Today, visitors are allowed to take tours of the mansion and its grounds.

the garden is a monument marking the graves of the president and his wife.

▷ Graceland

Elvis Presley was another Tennessee resident who became rich and famous. Presley was born in Tupelo, Mississippi, but moved to Tennessee as a young boy. In 1957, Presley bought Graceland, a beautiful Memphis mansion, for himself and his parents. It was his home until he died there on August 16, 1977. Graceland and the other Presley attractions are almost always crowded, especially around the anniversary of his death.

▲ *In 1957, Elvis Presley purchased Graceland for $102,500. Although Elvis passed away in 1977, the five-hundred-acre home was not open to the public until 1982. Within the first year of the mansion's opening, 300,000 visitors passed through its halls.*

Visitors may tour Graceland's first-floor kitchen, pool room, and living areas. On the grounds are other buildings, including offices and a trophy room which holds Presley's gold records.

Since his death, millions of Elvis fans have toured Graceland, then walked through the Sincerely Elvis Museum and the Elvis Presley Automobile Museum. Where else could you see "The King's" pink Cadillac? Visitors also crowd onto a pair of Presley's airplanes—the *Hound Dog II* and the *Lisa Marie*, one of the most luxurious jets ever built.

Great Smoky Mountains

There is really no smoke in the Great Smoky Mountains. What looks like smoke is really a thick moist mist that frequently clings to the mountains.

Great Smoky Mountains National Park covers more than 520,000 acres. Half of them are located in Tennessee, and the rest are in North Carolina. The Great Smokies are the highest mountain range in eastern North America.

The park has a greater variety of trees than grow in all of Europe. There are more than one hundred different types. Probably the park's most spectacular plant is the rhododendron, a big beautiful bush that blooms in June and July. Some of the bushes grow to heights of twenty feet. In places the bushes are so thick, it is impossible to get through them.

Great Smoky Mountains National Park is a wonderful place in which to wander. It has more than eight hundred miles of horse and foot trails. The scenery seems to improve the farther hikers get away from the main roads. The most beautiful waterfalls in the park are located deep in the

▲ *The Great Smoky Mountains National Park, covering over eight hundred square miles, is one of the largest protected areas in the East.*

forests. Visitors are welcome to fish and camp in many areas throughout the park. Hunting is not permitted.

▷ Opry Mills/The Grand Ole Opry

After all these years, the show is still going on in Nashville. The Grand Ole Opry is the longest running program in broadcasting. It has not missed a performance since 1925.

The program is performed in the Grand Ole Opry House, located on the Opryland grounds, which seats 4,400. During the summer, the seats are sold out weeks in advance. Fans know that some of country music's biggest names will be on hand for the Friday and Saturday night shows.

Opryland also includes river cruises, shopping, entertainment, and a hotel.

Dollywood

One of the most unique, and most popular amusement parks in Tennessee is Dollywood, located in Pigeon Forge. It is a project of country singer Dolly Parton.

The park has rides, including a big roller coaster called the Tennessee Tornado. It also has the Dolly Parton Museum and Jukebox Junction, a salute to the culture of the 1950s. Dollywood also pays tribute to mountain life through a series of craft shops. The Smoky Mountain Christmas celebration is held there annually.

Halls of Fame

Tennessee residents honor athletes and musicians in three well-known halls of fame. The Southern Gospel Music

The Country Music Hall of Fame inducted its first members in 1961. This award is the most prestigious in country music. The current Country Music Hall of Fame and Museum was opened on May 17, 2001, in downtown Nashville.

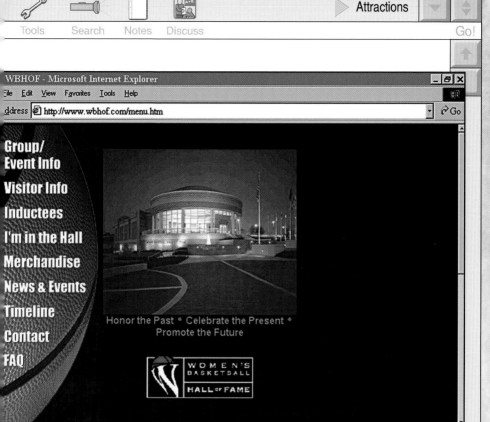

Group/
Event Info

Visitor Info

Inductees

I'm in the Hall

Merchandise

News & Events

Timeline

Contact

FAQ

Honor the Past • Celebrate the Present •
Promote the Future

WOMEN'S
BASKETBALL
HALL of FAME

Done   Internet

▲ *The Women's Basketball Hall of Fame is located in Knoxville, Tennessee. It preserves the history of women's basketball, beginning in 1892, when Smith College's Senda Berenson twisted the rules to make the game more "ladylike."*

Hall of Fame, in Dollywood, is dedicated to performers and writers who have influenced Southern religious music.

The Country Music Hall of Fame moved into a new facility in Nashville in 2001. Displays and movies honor the superstars of country music. On display is one of Elvis Presley's Cadillac automobiles. Another popular display is "Treasures of Hank Williams."

Knoxville is the home of the Women's Basketball Hall of Fame. Displays pay tribute to Senda Berenson, "the mother of women's basketball," and the All American Red

Heads, the first professional women's team. A giant 20,000-pound basketball is built into the side of the building. It is twenty feet in circumference.

National Civil Rights Museum

Rosa Parks is one of the heroes honored at the National Civil Rights Museum, in Memphis. The museum is housed in the Lorraine Motel, site of the 1968 assassination of Martin Luther King, Jr. Parks was the African-American woman who refused to give up her seat on a bus in 1955. Her action set off the Montgomery, Alabama, bus boycott and energized the civil rights movement. Other exhibits highlight court decisions, laws, and events involved in the long struggle to gain equal rights for all Americans.

Arenas and Stadiums

Memphis is also home to the Pyramid Arena. One of the most uniquely designed structures in the United States, the Pyramid is thirty-two stories high. It is in the shape of a pyramid like you would find in Egypt. The Pyramid is home to the Memphis Grizzlies of the NBA and the University of Memphis men's basketball team.

Overlooking downtown Nashville is the Coliseum, the home of the Tennessee Titans of the National Football League. The Titans share the stadium with Tennessee State University. In downtown Nashville, sports fans can find the Gaylord Entertainment Center, known simply as the GEC. The GEC is home to the Nashville Predators of the National Hockey League.

Interesting People

Many interesting and famous people are either natives of Tennessee or have called it home. From American Indians to country music performers, Tennesseans can be proud of these sons and daughters.

▶ Sequoyah

In 1776, the year the American Revolution began, Sequoyah, a Cherokee Indian, was born near Tuskeegee. As more and more white settlers moved into Tennessee, Sequoyah moved to Georgia and became a silversmith. When he saw that other smiths signed their work, he decided to learn to read and write so he could sign, too. However, the Cherokee language did not have any letters, so it could not be written. So he learned English, but he began working on a Cherokee writing system.

After twelve years of working on a Cherokee alphabet, Sequoyah introduced the eighty-five letters to the Cherokee nation. Within months, thousands of Cherokees were literate.

After many years, Sequoyah came up with eighty-five letters for a written Cherokee alphabet. In 1821, the Cherokee nation adopted his alphabet.

Sequoyah later represented the views of his people in Washington, D.C. The huge sequoia trees and California's Sequoia National Park are named in his honor.

David "Davy" Crockett

In 1786, David Crockett was born in the Tennessee wilderness. When he was a child, his father built and ran a tavern in Jefferson County. Travelers probably told the boy many stories about life on the frontier.

When he was thirteen, Crockett got into a fight at school. To avoid a beating from his father, he ran away from home—for two and a half years. Most of the time he spent working in Virginia.

After returning home, Crockett became an expert marksman. After he married and moved deep into the frontier, he used his skill to provide food for his family.

People loved listening to stories of his adventures fighting American Indians and hunting animals. Some

David Crockett lives on in history as a heroic frontiersman. His strong, charismatic personality not only made him a legendary storyteller, but it also helped him in his career as a statesman.

people felt that Crockett made up some of his adventures. However, Crockett's Tennessee neighbors respected him enough to elect him to the state legislature and the U.S. Congress. After losing the election for what would have been his fourth term in Congress, he went west to join Texans in their fight for independence from Mexico. He was killed with 189 other men at the Battle of the Alamo.

Andrew Jackson

Andrew Jackson was the first American president to grow up on the frontier.[1] He was born in the Waxhaw District of South Carolina. A few weeks before he was born, Andrew's father died. Andrew's mother and two brothers died in the Revolutionary War, leaving him an orphan at age fourteen.

Like the other two United States presidents from Tennessee, Andrew Jackson was not born in the state but moved there in 1786, at the age of nineteen.

Jackson was an intelligent boy. In 1776, when he was only nine, his neighbors chose him to read the Declaration of Independence to them. However, he was also a stubborn boy with quite a temper. While he was serving in the militia four years later, he was captured by the British, who ordered him to clean their boots. The boy refused—even when the commander drew his sword. The angry man cut him badly by striking him in the head and hand. When he grew up, Jackson was still famous for his temper.

The future president moved to Nashville in 1788 soon after he became a lawyer. He was elected to the Tennessee constitutional convention and then to the U.S. Senate. Later he became a judge.

Jackson first gained the attention of the nation as a military commander during the War of 1812. His men defeated the Creek Indians at the Battle of Horseshoe Bend in 1814. On January 8, 1815, Jackson's troops defeated the British at the Battle of New Orleans. The victories made him a national hero. He was elected president in 1828 and 1832.

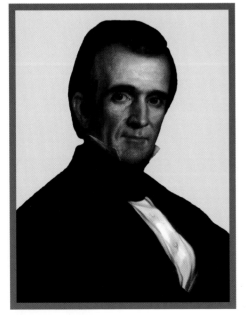

◁ James K. Polk, the nation's eleventh president, moved to Columbia, Tennessee, as a boy in 1806. He served one term in the Tennessee House of Representatives, fourteen years as a congressman from the state, and one term as Tennessee's governor before becoming president in 1845.

James K. Polk

Like his friend Andrew Jackson, James K. Polk moved to Tennessee after he became a lawyer. He served the state as a congressman and governor.

In 1844, Polk was not widely known, but Jackson convinced the Democratic Party to nominate him for president. Polk was elected and served just one term. During that time, the country doubled in size. Texas was annexed, and much of the Oregon Territory was obtained from the British. Polk also guided the country through the Mexican-American War. The treaty that ended the war gave the country much of the land which is now the Southwestern United States.

Andrew Johnson

Even when his state seceded and the Civil War began in 1861, Tennessee Senator Andrew Johnson continued to serve in Washington. After the state fell to Union troops, President Abraham Lincoln appointed him military governor of Tennessee.

In 1864, Johnson was elected vice president. When Lincoln was assassinated a few months later, Johnson became president. In 1868, disagreements with Congress resulted in his impeachment by the House of Represen-tatives. The Senate came within one vote of convicting him and removing him from office.

Wilma Rudolph

After being born prematurely in 1940 in Clarksville, Tennessee, Wilma Rudolph was a sick little girl. She had measles, mumps, scarlet fever, chicken pox, double pneu-monia, and finally polio. The polio made her left leg weak.

Because Wilma was African American, Tennessee's white hospitals refused to treat her. For two years, her mother, Blanche, drove her fifty miles twice a week to hospital for African Americans in Nashville.

Physical therapy made it possible for her to walk only with corrective shoes. When she was twelve years old, Wilma threw away those shoes and ran. In high school, she became a star basketball player. At Tennessee State University, she was a track superstar.

With the whole world watching, Rudolph became the first American woman to win three Olympic gold medals. In the Summer Olympics at Rome in 1960, she won the 100- and 200-meter dashes, then ran on the winning 400-meter relay squad. She was recognized as the fastest woman in the world.

▷ Alex Haley

When he was a boy growing up in Henning, Tennessee, Alex Haley heard family stories about his ancestor Kunta Kinte, who had been captured in Africa and brought to the United States as a slave.

After he grew up, Haley spent years researching his family's history. He eventually discovered the village in Africa where Kunta Kinte had lived. He put his family's history together in *Roots*, one of the best-selling books in history. *Roots* also became the most-watched miniseries in television history in January 1977. Haley is also well-known for writing *The Autobiography of Malcolm X*.

History

People have lived in the area that would become Tennessee for over thirteen thousand years. The first known group is called the Paleo Indians. They lived in camps, gathered wild foods, and hunted large animals. The next group was known as the Archaic peoples. They were hunters and gatherers for many centuries until they learned to plant food and domesticate animals such as turkeys.

About two thousand years ago, the Woodland culture appeared. They farmed corn, squash, and bean crops. In addition, they made pottery and built burial

▲ The Big South Fork of the Cumberland River provides visitors with many recreational activities, including whitewater rafting, canoeing, kayaking, camping, horseback riding, hiking, and more.

mounds—dirt hills that rose as high as seventy-two feet. The next group to arrive, the Mississippians, had a complex society with big towns, temple mounds, decorated shells, pottery, copper, and agriculture. Living in Tennessee from A.D. 900 to 1600, they traded with other natives that lived as far as present-day Florida and Wyoming. The Mississippians disappeared after 1600, and later settlers found their mounds a mystery. Many think the Cherokee, Creek, and Chickasaw Indians are the descendants of these cultures.

Explorers and Settlers

The first white men seen by Tennessee's American Indians were Spanish explorers led by Hernando de Soto from 1540 to 1541. There was no additional contact with Europeans until 1673 when James Needham and Gabriel Arthur explored eastern Tennessee for England. At almost the same time two Frenchmen, Louis Joliet and Jacques Marquette, made their way through the western part of the state.

In 1682, Robert Cavelier, Sieur de la Salle, the great French explorer, claimed the entire Mississippi Valley, including Tennessee, for France. On the Chickasaw Bluffs near the present site of Memphis, he built Fort Prud'homme. Thirty-two years later, Charles Charleville established a French trading post at French Lick, near the site that would one day become Nashville.

The French were mainly interested in fur trading, not establishing settlements. Meanwhile, North Carolina, Virginia, and the other British colonies located east of Tennessee continued to grow. After France lost the French and Indian War in 1763, all of the region east of the Mississippi River belonged to Great Britain.

A New Country

Tennessee was considered part of the colony of North Carolina when settlers began heading west over the mountains. They usually followed the Wilderness Trail from Virginia through Kentucky. Tennessee's earliest settlements were established along the Holston and Nolichucky rivers and Watauga Lake.

The settlers, known as the Wataugans, made history by setting up their own independent government. They did not ask the king or his representatives for permission, and the British authorities were angered by this. When the American Revolution began in 1776, settlers from Tennessee helped defeat British troops at King's Mountain, South Carolina. Five years later, the peace treaty was signed. The region that would become the

▲ *There was much wilderness in Tennessee for frontiersmen to explore. Sites, such as Baby Falls (pictured here), awaited them.*

state of Tennessee was now part of the United States of America.

The State of Franklin

Just as the Revolution began, the Watauga settlers agreed to officially become part of North Carolina. Their settlements were known as the Washington District. After the war, however, the Wataugans no longer wanted to be part of North Carolina. They decided to form their own state named in honor of Benjamin Franklin. In 1784, three counties joined to become the new state of Franklin. John "Nolichucky Jack" Sevier was elected governor.

Franklin was never officially a state. North Carolina still claimed the land and tried to collect taxes there. Its representatives fought in Congress to prevent Franklin's admission to the Union. After four years, the people of Franklin gave up. They allowed their land to become part of North Carolina again. Sevier was elected to the North Carolina Senate.

Tennessee was only a part of North Carolina for only two more years. The land then became part of a territory set up by the national government. In 1796, Tennessee was admitted to the Union as the sixteenth state, and Sevier was elected governor.

American Indians and African Americans

Richard Henderson wanted to get rich by selling land in Tennessee and Kentucky. He set up the Transylvania Land Company to handle his transactions. He convinced a group of Cherokee chiefs to sell him 20 million acres of land for roughly fifty thousand dollars. It is one of the largest land deals in the history of the United States.

Chief Dragging Canoe knew it was a terrible deal for his people. He tried to talk the other chiefs out of signing the agreement. They would not listen. The papers were signed. Dragging Canoe organized attacks on the whites, but the settlers did not leave. It was the American Indians who finally had to go. They gave up even more land in the one-sided Chickasaw Purchase deal in 1818. Finally, in 1830, President Andrew Jackson convinced Congress to pass the Indian Removal Act. In 1838, fourteen thousand Cherokee were forced to leave Tennessee for new land in Oklahoma. Almost four thousand of them died on the way in what has been called the Trail of Tears.

When Tennessee joined the Union, most of the African Americans who lived there were slaves. They worked mostly in the middle part of the state. African Americans who were not slaves had the right to vote until 1834 when Tennessee passed a new state constitution. After that it was illegal for African Americans to vote.

The Civil War

When the nation split apart in 1861, Tennessee itself was divided. People who lived in the eastern part of the state, where there were few slaves, supported President Abraham Lincoln and the

This cannon overlooks the Civil War battlefield at Chattanooga, where, in November 1863, the Union Army claimed victory.

Union. The people who lived in the other parts of the state supported the South, or the Confederate States. Tennessee finally voted to leave the Union on June 8, 1861, but Andrew Johnson, one of Tennessee's senators, refused to leave Washington, D.C. He said he was still a senator since a state had no right to secede. President Lincoln later appointed him the state's military governor.

One of the Civil War's bloodiest battles was fought in the southwestern part of the state at Shiloh in 1862. The North won several battles in 1862, opening most of the state to Yankee troops. A year later, Union soldiers took Chattanooga in a fierce battle.

After the Union won the war, Tennessee became the first Confederate state to rejoin the Union in 1868. By then, Andrew Johnson was president.

Rebuilding

The fighting left much of Tennessee in ruins. The years after the Civil War were very difficult for the people. Forty years passed before the state's farms were back in full production again.

The Radical Republicans who controlled the state after the war wanted to punish those who had supported the South. Many white residents lost the right to vote. African Americans, however, were permitted to vote. The Radicals were voted out of office in 1869, and things returned mostly to the way they had always been.

Then the state was hit by a terrible epidemic of yellow fever. Memphis had less than twenty thousand people, but more than five thousand of them died from the disease in 1878.

On a positive note, factories and mining operations were steadily established in Tennessee. Highways and

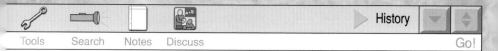
railroads were also being built throughout most of the state. These created much needed jobs.

Tennessee Valley Authority

The Great Depression of the 1930s was a disaster for Tennessee and the rest of the nation. People lost jobs and had little money and sometimes no food. President Franklin D. Roosevelt's New Deal proposed programs designed to improve the economy and the lives of Americans. One of the most successful programs was the Tennessee Valley Authority (TVA).

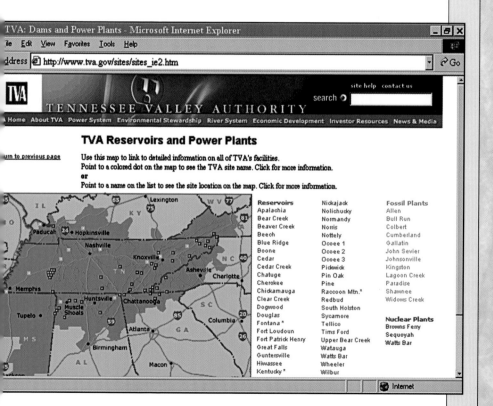

The Tennessee Valley Authority was a program enacted under President Franklin Delano Roosevelt's New Deal. TVA operates in, and services a total of seven states.

The TVA was designed to build dams to control the Tennessee River and to harness its power. Thirty-nine dams were built. They prevented flooding and made it easier for boats to use the river. The most important effect was making cheap electric power available for the first time to thousands of Tennessee families. Electricity produced by the spinning turbines inside the dams, as well as by steam plants, produced power for the entire area. The TVA also provided the people of Tennessee with thousands of jobs.

Civil Rights

Much like other Southern states at the time, Tennessee's laws discriminated against African-American citizens. African-American children were segregated, or separated, and put into inferior schools compared to the schools for white children. Laws were passed that made it difficult for African Americans to vote.

During the 1950s and 1960s, such laws began to change. Segregation and discrimination were made illegal. Tennessee's African Americans could now vote, and many have also been elected to office.

One of the most terrible events of the civil rights struggle occurred in Memphis. Martin Luther King, Jr., perhaps the most important African-American leader of the time, was assassinated there in 1968. He was in the city to support striking garbage workers.

Tennessee Today

More people in the twenty-first century live in Tennessee's cities, or urban areas, than in the country. People have been drawn to the cities to work in service industries, such as stores, restaurants, hospitals, and banks. They also

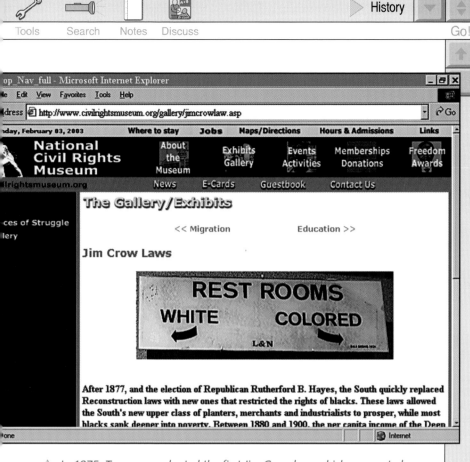

nday, February 03, 2003   **Where to stay   Jobs   Maps/Directions   Hours & Admissions   Links**

National Civil Rights Museum   About the Museum   Exhibits Gallery   Events Activities   Memberships Donations   Freedom Awards

lrightsmuseum.org   News   E-Cards   Guestbook   Contact Us

The Gallery/Exhibits

ces of Struggle
lery

<< Migration   Education >>

Jim Crow Laws

REST ROOMS
WHITE   COLORED
L&N

After 1877, and the election of Republican Rutherford B. Hayes, the South quickly replaced Reconstruction laws with new ones that restricted the rights of blacks. These laws allowed the South's new upper class of planters, merchants and industrialists to prosper, while most blacks sank deeper into poverty. Between 1880 and 1900, the per capita income of the Deep

▲ In 1875, Tennessee adopted the first Jim Crow law, which segregated blacks from whites on wharves and trains, and in depots. The National Civil Rights Museum exists to increase public understanding of the civil rights movement.

come for manufacturing jobs, especially in automobile factories. Almost ninety-one thousand Tennessee farms, however, still grow crops, raise cattle, and produce hardwood lumber. Tourism and entertainment are also major employers for people in the state. As the year 2000 began, Tennessee was enjoying one of the most prosperous economic times in state history.[1] Tennesseans hope their state continues to grow.

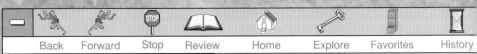
Chapter Notes

Tennessee Facts

1. Tennessee's six state songs are: "My Homeland, Tennessee" (words by Nell Grayson Taylor, music by Roy Lamont Smith); "When It's Iris Time in Tennessee" (words and music by Willa Waid Newan); "My Tennessee" (words and music by Francis Hannah Tranum); "Tennessee Waltz" (words by Redd Stewart, music by Pee Wee King); "Rocky Top" (words and music by Boudleaux and Felice Bryant).

Chapter 1. The Music of Tennessee

1. Arnold Shaw, "Grand Ole Opry," *Southern Music Network,* 1997–2003, <http://www.southernmusic.net /grandoleopry.htm> (April 8, 2003).

2. Gaylord Entertainment, "Grand Ole Opry to Return to Ryman Auditorium," *Opry News and Information,* October 20, 1999, <http://www.opry.com/04_info/04_leadstory/ pressrelease.asp?prID=90> (April 8, 2003).

3. The Arts Report, "Elvis tops the album charts," *CBC Art News,* March 10, 2002, <http://www.cbc.ca/artsCanada/ stories/elvis031002> (April 8, 2003).

Chapter 4. Interesting People

1. Mary Beth Norton, David M. Katzman, Paul D. Escott, et. al., *A People and A Nation: Volume I* (Boston: Houghton Mifflin Company, 1990), p. 356.

Chapter 5. History

1. State of Tennessee Publications Division, "Modern Tennessee," *A History of Tennessee,* 2002, <http://www.state .tn.us/sos/bluebook/online/section6/modern.pdf> (April 8, 2003).

Further Reading

Alagna, Magdalena. *Elvis Presley.* New York: The Rosen Publishing Group, Incorporated, 2001.

Aylesworth, Thomas G. and Virginia L. *The Southeast: Georgia, Kentucky, Tennessee.* Broomall, Penn.: Chelsea House Publishers, 1995.

Ching, Jacqueline. *The Assassination of Martin Luther King, Jr.* New York: The Rosen Publishing Group, Incorporated, 2001.

Kent, Deborah. *Tennessee.* Danbury, Conn.: Scholastic Library Publishing, 2001.

Peck, Barbara. *Tennessee: The Volunteer State.* Milwaukee, WI: Gareth Stevens Incorporated, 2002.

Ruth, Amy. *Wilma Rudolph.* Minneapolis: Lerner Publishing Group, 1999.

Sanford, William R. and Carl R. Green. *Davy Crockett: Defender of the Alamo.* Berkeley Heights, N.J., 1996.

Shumate, Jane. Sequoyah: *Inventor of the Cherokee Alphabet.* Broomall, Penn.: Chelsea House Publishers, 1994.

Thompson, Kathleen. *Tennessee.* Austin, Tex.: Raintree Publishers, 1996.

Index